TABLE OF CONTENTS

LEGAL NOTES AND DISCLAIMER

content and information in this book has been provided for educational and entertainment purposes only.

The content and information contained in this book has been compiled from sources deemed reliable, and it is accurate to the best of the Author's knowledge, information and belief. However, the Author cannot guarantee its accuracy and validity and cannot be held liable for any errors and/or omissions. Furthermore, changes can be periodically made to this book as and when needed. Where appropriate and/or necessary, you must consult a professionalbefore using any of the suggested remedies, techniques, or information in this book.

INTRODUCTION

This e-book welcomes all those who are interested in learning and working with some of the most known numerical methods using MATLAB. Thiswriting will also prove useful for those who havehard time intercepting how MATLAB works. Here, you will have a chance to understand and learnstep-by-step how MATLAB works and also practiceon the methods that will be described. Also youare invited to copypaste the code and execute it.I wish you a pleasant reading and I welcome you at the magical world of numerical analysis.

CHAPTER 1. CALCULATING VALUES OF FUNCTION

At first, glance, calculating the value of the function at a certain point is not a hard problem. The simplest way is to plug the number into the formula. An example follows:

```
syms x ;
y=x^2  +2* x+  1 ;
subs (y, 3 )
```

This is very simple. We define a symbolic variable named x. Then, using this variable we define the

equation $y = x^2 + 2x + 1$, which is symbolic too.

Finally, using the command $subs$, we compute the value of the equation when x is equal to three. The output would be 16.

Of course, there is a simpler way. You can just run the following piece of code:

```
y  =  (3) ^ 2  +  2 * ( 3 )  +  1;
```

Again, y is 16.

However, sometimes, this straightforward approach is not efficient. For polynomials, a better approach is using Horner's scheme. Horner's scheme is a method for approximating the roots of a polynomial or calculating polynomials. This is how it works: Given the polynomial

$$p(x) = \sum_{i=0}^{n} a_i x^i = a_0 + a_1 x + \cdots + a_n x^n \quad (1.1)$$

We wish to evaluate the function's value at a specific
x_0. To accomplish that, we set the following sequenceof constants:

$b_n := a_n$

$b_{N-1:} = a_{n-1} + b_n x_0$

$$\ldots \qquad\qquad (1.2)$$

$b_0 := a_0 + b_1 x_0$

Then, b_0 is the value of $p(x_0)$. To see how this works, note that the polynomial can be written in the form $p(x) = a_0 + x(a_1 + x(a_2 + \cdots + x(a_{n-1} + a_n x)))$.

$$(1.3)$$

Thus, by iterating and substituting b_i in the expression

$$p(x_0) = a_0 + x_0 \left(a_1 + x_0 \left(a_2 + \cdots + x_0 \left(a_{n-1} + b_n x_0\right)\right)\right)$$

$$= a_0 + x_0 \left(a_1 + x_0 \left(a_2 + \cdots + x_0 \left(b_{n-1}\right)\right)\right)$$

$$= \ldots$$

$$= a_0 + x_0 \left(b_1\right)$$

$$= b_0.$$

In order to simulate this process in MATLAB using the previous polynomial, we just execute the following code:

```
a  =   [1    2    1];
b  =   zeros(3,1);

x0 = 3;
```

```
b ( 1 ) = 1 ;

f o r i = 2 : length ( a )
        b ( i ) = a ( i ) + b ( i−1)∗ x0 ;
end
```

Here, we have defined an array a, where we store the coefficients that are multiplied at each power of the polynomial. Then, we set an array that will store the new coefficients, the point at which we would like to calculate the value of the function. We set the first cell of the new coefficients at the last value of the new coefficients. Then, by using the formula described above, we calculate the matrix b. The last cell of matrix b holds the value of the function at the specified point.

One more thing we have to take control of, when we use MATLAB in order to compute the value of a function at a point, is the round-off error. Round-off errors, in simple terms, is the difference between the estimated value of the function and the real one.

Imagine we have the function $y = \sqrt{x}$. When x is equal to 4, then y is 2. When x is 16, y is 4.

When x is 2, then y has an infinite number of digits. These digits cannot be represented in any programming language, since infinite digits mean infinite memory. The difference between the value stored in a variable in MATLAB and the real value is the round-off error. When a sequence of calculations subject to rounding error is made, errors may accumulate, sometimes dominating the calculation. In order to avoid this situation, we have to represent infinite length numberswith more digits. In MATLAB, we do it like so:

```
format    long
y  =  sqrt(2)
```

Now y is represented using 16 decimal digits.

CHAPTER 2. *INTERPOLATION, EXTRAPOLATION, REGRESSION*

Our next goal is to understand and implement in MATLAB interpolation, extrapolation, and regression. These 3 techniques may have similarities in what they mean or how they can help us solving a problem, but if we look closely, we will find significant differences that make these techniques unique.Let us start with interpolation. Interpolation is a method of constructing new data points within the range of a discrete set of known data points. In simple terms, this is a technique for finding values of an unknown function at a point between given values of points of this function. For example, we have the function $y = x^2$ and we know the values for $x = -2,-1,0,1,2$ and we want to find the value for $x = -1.5,-0.5,0.5,1.5$. We suppose that the function y is unknown, so we cannot just plug the points and find the value. So we will use interpolation. Below, we see this example implemented in MATLAB.

```
x = [-2 -1 0 1 2];
```

```
y = x.^2;
```

```
u = [-1.5 -0.5 0.5 1.5];
```

```
vi = interp1(x,y,u);
```

Let's take a look at this piece of code. Variable x holds the points of the function that we will knowof. Variable y holds the actual values of the known points since it is equal to x^2. Variable u holds the points when we want to estimate the unknown function. To do so, we use the command $interp1$, that given the known points, the known values, and the

unknown points computes the new values. Let us
see the result:

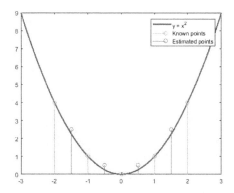

The blue line represents the function $y = x^2$ and the
green vertical lines represent the known values of

the function. Using the command described above,we estimate the values for the points in between and we plot the using the red vertical lines. As we can see, our estimate is close to the real value. MATLAB gives us the option to use the technique of interpolation to estimate points of functions of more than one variable. Anyone interested can easily find this by researching.

Our next stop is extrapolation. Very similar to interpolation, extrapolation is used to find values of an unknown function at a point which is outside the given points. This has many applications, such as estimating the future value of a function given all its previous values. For instance, if our function is the price of a share at Wall Street, then one can use extrapolation to estimate the price of the share the next day.

Let us make a small change in the example we saw before. Suppose that we have the unknown function $y = x^2$ and this time we know the values for the points

$x = -2, -1, 0, 1$. We wish to estimatefor Additive white Gaussian Noise. Naturally, this function adds white noise, normally distributed, to every sample of the $y = x$ with SNR equal to 5. SNR stands for signal-to-noise ratio and is a term widely used in telecommunications. SRN equal to 5 means that the energy of the signal is 5 times greater than the energy of the noise. Finally, we use the MATLAB function regression, whose first parameter is the x-axis and the second is the noisy data. Last but not least, we plot the result and what we get is this:

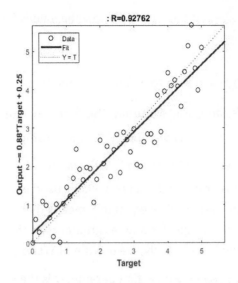

We can see that the estimated curve fits the data supplied and it is close to the actual function we had defined. Here, we must denote that the function we used is for *linear regression*. Asalways, there is much more to see if someone wants to understand regression deeply.

CHAPTER 3. *EQUATIONS AND SYSTEMS OF EQUATIONS*

Another fundamental problem in numerical analysis is computing the solution of some given equation. Two cases are commonly distinguished, depending on whether the equation is linear or not. For instance, the equation $2x + 5 = 3$ is linear while $2x^2 + 5 = 3$ is not.

Once again, solving an equation can be simplifiedusing MATLAB. A demonstration of solving an equation using MATLAB is provided below:

syms x

```
eqn = ( 2* x – 5 == 3 ) ;
solx = solve ( eqn , x )
```

Let us try to understand this code. At first, a symbolic variable is defined using the command $syms\,x$. Then, we define the equation we want to solve. The variable eqn holds the equation, which is stated in the parenthesis. Here, the double equal denotes equality and is a logical operator. When we use single equal, we denote assignment. So finally, variable eqn holds the linear equation we used before. Last, by using the command $solve$, which is a build-in command in MATLAB, we find the x that satisfies the equation. The parameters of the command, in this case, are two. The first is the symbolic representation of the target equation and the second is the variable with respect to which we will solve the equation. The result we get is 4 that would be the same if we solved the equation by hand. Of course, this is just an example. MATLAB can cope with equations of much higher order and complexity, such as equations of complex numbers, trigonometric functions, multi-variable functions and much more.

We saw that no matter how complex an equation can be, MATLAB always has an answer. However, MATLAB also gives us the option to tackle systems of equations. There are two approaches we will examine here. The first is by using the build in function of MATLAB $_{solve,}$ and the other is by using linear algebra with MATLAB.Let us consider the pair of equations $2x - y = 0$ and $x-y = 1$. It is widely known that the pair of $_{x,y}$ that satisfies this system of equations corresponds to the point in the Cartesian field where those two lines meet. This is how we solve this system with MATLAB:

```
syms   x  y

eqn = [ 2* x – y == 0 , x – y == 1 ] ;
solx = solve ( eqn , [ x y ] )
```

Once again, we define 2 symbolic variables x,y. Next, we define our equation, only this time, since we have a system we want to solve, we set the variable *eqn* to tobe a 2-by-1 matrix that holds the symbolic equations. Finally, we use *solve* to find the solution for this system of equations concerning x,y.

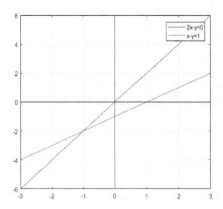

As we explained before, the solution is the point where the two lines meet, as we see at the figure above. This is the first way we can solve a system of equations in MATLAB.

The second way is using linear algebra. We have to create the model $Az = b$ where A is a n-by-n matrix holding the coefficients of the variables, z is the vector of variables and b is the vector that holds the constants. In the example we saw before we have that:

$$A = \begin{bmatrix} 2 & -1 \\ 1 & -1 \end{bmatrix}, z = \begin{bmatrix} x \\ y \end{bmatrix}, b = \begin{bmatrix} 0 \\ 1 \end{bmatrix}$$

The solution to the equation $Az = b$ is given by multiplying with the inverse of the matrix A from the left:

$$Az = b$$
$$A^{-1}Az = A^{-1}b \qquad\qquad (3.2)$$
$$z = A^{-1}b$$

The implementation in MATLAB is as follows:

```
A =     [2  –1;
         1  –1];
b  =  [0  ;  1];
Ainv = inv (A ) ;

z = Ainv*b ;
```

At first, we define the matrices A and b as we did above. Next, we use the command inv that uses as input the matrix A and returns its inverse. Finally, we multiply the inverse matrix with the constant vector.

Once again, we get the system solution.

CHAPTER 4. *EIGENVALUE AND SINGULAR VALUE DECOMPOSITION*

Several important problems can be phrasedregarding eigenvalue decompositions or singular value decompositions. This is why these two techniques are two of the most popular tools in numerical analysis. Mainlyit is about decomposing matrices tothe product of other matrices each of which contains hidden information about the initial one.

In linear algebra, eigenvalue decomposition is the factorization of a matrix into a canonical form, whereby the matrix is representedregarding its eigenvalues and eigenvectors. Only diagonalizable matrices can be factorized in this way. A (non-zero) vector v of dimension N is an eigenvector of a square N-by-N matrix A if it satisfies the linear equation

$$Av = \lambda v \qquad (4.1)$$

Where λ is a scalar, termed the eigenvalue corresponding to v. Now, if the eigenvectors are linearly independent, meaning that no eigenvector can be written as a linear combination of other eigenvectors, then matrix A can be factorized as:

$$A = Q\Lambda Q^{-1}, \qquad (4.2)$$

Where Q is the square N-by-N matrix whose $i{-}th$ column is the eigenvector q_i of A and Λ is the diagonal matrix whose diagonal elements are the corresponding eigenvalues.

Decomposing a matrix to its eigenvalues and eigenvectors can prove a tough task if done by hand. Fortunately, MATLAB has a simple solution. Below, we demonstrate the use of the MATLAB command *eig*.

```
A  =    randn ( 1 0 , 1 0 ) ;
[Q, L]   =   eig ( A ) ;
```

This piece of code is pretty simple to understand. There are two steps. The first is to generate a random N-by-N matrix, where in this case N is equal to 10. Next, by using the command *eig*, we have successfully performed eigenvalue decomposition. Command *eig* has one parameter, and that is the rectangular matrix we want to decompose, in this case, A. The output of this function is 2 matrices. The first matrix Q

contains the eigenvectors of A and the second one contains the corresponding eigenvalues on its diagonal. Matrix L is a diagonal matrix, meaning that only its diagonal has non zero elements, in this case, the eigenvalues. As an exercise, you can run these 2 lines in MATLAB and then try this:

```
B  = Q * L * inv ( Q ) ;
A == B
```

Essentially, what we are doing here, is that we compose the original matrix A by using the outcomes from the eigenvalue decomposition. The last command compares the original matrix to the recomposed one. The outcome of this command should be 1.

Note: Sometimes the *eig* function might return complex values, even if the original input matrix is real. This means, that when trying to recompose the original matrix using Q and L the new matrix will be complicated too. This does not mean we did something

wrong. If you take a closer look at the new matrix, you should see that the imaginary part is zero and the real part is the same as the original matrix.

Now let us take a look at the singular value decomposition. Singular value decomposition (SVD) is a factorization of a real or complex matrix. It is the generalization of the eigenvalue decomposition of a definitesemidefiniteregular matrix (for example, a symmetric matrix with positive eigenvalues) to any m-by-n matrix. It has many useful applications in signal processing and statistics.

Formally, the singular-value decomposition of an m-by-n real or complex matrix A is a factorization of the form USV^*, where U is an m-by-m real or complex unitary matrix, S is a m-by-n rectangular diagonal matrix with non-negative real numbers on the diagonal, and V is an n-by-n real or complex unitary matrix. The diagonal entries s_i of S are known as the singular values of A. The columns of U, and the columns of V are called the left-singular vectors and right-singular vectors of A, respectively.

The singular-value decomposition can be computed using the following observations:

- The left-singular vectors of A are a set of orthonormal eigenvectors of AA^*.

- The right-singular vectors of A are a set of orthonormal eigenvectors of A^*A.

- The non-zero singular values of A (found on the diagonal entries of S) are the square roots of the non-zero eigenvalues of both

A^*A and

$AA*$.

So it is pretty clear that singular value decomposition is close to eigenvalue decomposition. Let's see how we can implement this process using MATLAB:

```
A = randn( 1 5 , 1 0 ) ;
[U, S , V]    =   svd (A ) ;
```

As we can see the code is straightforward. First, we generate a random matrix 15-by-10 and we call the function svd. This function has only one parameter, which is the random matrix A. Its output it's3 matrices that correspond to the 3 matrices U, S, and V that we described above. Again, as we did in eigenvalue decomposition, we can verify that the matrices we got are correct, by trying to compose the initial matrix by using those 3. To do that, we will execute this command: B = U∗ S ∗V ' ;

We just multiply the 3 matrices. We have to observe that we do not multiply with V, but with its transpose matrix. When we have complex data, we have to multiply with the *Hermitian* of matrix V. A transpose matrix is a matrix whose we take its columns,and we use them as rows. A Hermitian matrix is one whose columns have become rows but also all the cells of the matrix are replaced with their conjugate.

If we compare the matrix B with the initial matrix$A$, we will see that they are equal. This is something we would expect.

As we saw before, one can calculate the 3 matrices given by the SVD by computing the matrices AA^*

and A^*A and then performing eigenvalue decomposition. However, here, it is really important to denote that the eigenvalue decomposition can be performed only on rectangular matrices, while the singular valuedecomposition can be performed on any matrix, no matter its size.

It is pretty clear at this point that MATLAB is a potent tool that makes life easier when it comes to matrix manipulation.

CHAPTER
5.OPTIMIZATION

Optimization problems ask for the point at which a given function is maximized (or minimized). Often, the point also has to satisfy some constraints. The field of optimization is further split into several subfields, depending on the form of the objective function and the constraint. For instance, linear programming deals with the case that both the objective function and the constraints are linear. A famous method in linear programming is the simplex method.

The method of Lagrange multipliers can be used to reduce optimization problems with constraints to unconstrained optimization problems. Since this is an e-book for beginners, we are just going to scratch the surface of optimization.

Our primary focus will be on minimizing functions using MATLAB. However, one can quickly maximize functions by minimizing the opposite function. We will divide the optimization problems into two categories. The first one will be the unconstrained optimization and the second will be the optimization given some constraints.

First, we will discuss unconstrained optimization problems. In simple terms, minimizing the value of a function where x can take values everywhere on the x-axis. Let's consider a simple example in MATLAB:

```
fun = @( x ) ( x –2)^2 + 1 ;
x0 = –5;
x_opt=fminsearch( fun , x0 ) ;
```

Actually, it is not that hard to intercept this piece of code. First, we define a function of x, (denoted @(x) in the code) and then we express the function. It is pretty similar as to when we defined symbolic functions. The function we are asked to minimize this time is $(x - 2)^2 + 1$. We are going to skip the second line and go straight to the last line.

The command *fminsearch* takes as input two things. The first is the function it is asked to be minimized. The second is the point from which the command will start searching from. This point is defined at the second line $x_0 = 5$.

By running this code, we will see that variable x_{opt} will take the value 2. It is important to denote that function *fminsearch* returns the point when the function is minimized and not the value of the function. If we want to compute the value the function takes at this point, we can follow one of the guidelines described in chapter 1.

Below, we see the visualization of this process. There is a straight line from the optimal point to the minimum value of the function, that we calculated using the process above.

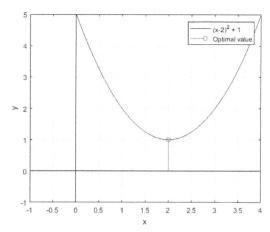

Now that we understood unconstrained optimization, we will talk about constrained optimization. The term constrain means that x can only take values on a specific range in the x-axis. Let us consider the previous example but this time, x can range from 3 to 4.5. Let's take a look at the MATLAB code that minimizes the function:

```
fun    = @( x ) ( x –2)^2   +  1 ;
x1 = 3 ;
x2 = 4 . 5 ;
x_opt = fminbnd( fun , x1 , x2 ) ;
```

Again, we have a symbolic function and variables $x1$ and $x2$ define the range x will take values in. In this case, as mentioned before, $x1$ is equal to 3 and $x2$ is equal to 4.5.

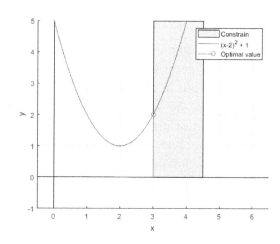

Finally, we use the function *fminbnd* that uses the function described and the range for the constrain and generates the optimal point of the function.

As we see in the figure above, the optimal point is different from the optimal point in the previous problem. We can see that when x is equal to 3, the function takes the minimum value in the range specified.

As always, it is important to stress out the fact that things can get very complex when talking about optimization. If someone wants to dive a little bit deeper, he can try minimizing multivariable functions or use constraints in more than one dimensions. Even though it is a difficult subject, it is fascinating and developing with a massive area of applications.

CHAPTER 6. *EVALUATING INTEGRALS*

Numerical integration asks for the value of a definite integral. Popular methods use one of the Newton-Cotes formulas (like the midpoint rule or Simpson's rule) or Gaussian quadrature. These methods rely on a "divide and conquer" strategy, whereby an integral on a relatively large set is broken down into integrals on smaller sets. In higher dimensions,

where these methods become prohibitively expensive regarding computational effort, one may use Monte

Carlo or quasi-Monte Carlo methods (see Monte 39

Carlo integration), or, in modestly large dimensions, the method of sparse grids. However, these methods are advanced,and since this e-book refers to beginners, we will not use them. Instead, we will use MATLAB to make things easier.

Often, a definite integral is interpreted as the area below the graph of a function from one point to another. For instance, let's consider the integral of the function $y = x$ from 0 to 3. This is pretty simple. All we have to do is calculate the area of the triangle formed from the lines $x = y, y = 0, x = 3$. However, as we see in the figure below, the area is a simple triangle. The area of the triangle is given by multiplying the two perpendicular sides and then dividing by 2. In this case, the area is 4.5. Let's try to solve this using the MATLAB built-in function *integral.*

```
fun = @( x ) x
q  =  integral ( fun , 0 , 3 )
```

First, we define the symbolic function $y = x$. Then

by using the function *integral* and we set as input the function and the range of the integral we get the final result. If we execute this 2 commands the result, we will get is 4.5.

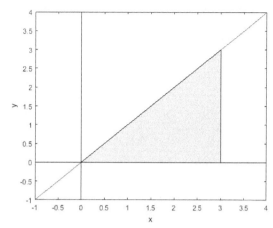

This was an easy example. Here we could compute the integral by hand and still get a correct result without going through much trouble. What is really interesting and difficult if done by hand, is computing integrals of non-linear function such as $y = x^2 + 1$. Here, we will need help from MATLAB. Now, we visualize the area below the function $y = x^2 + 1$ from -1 to 1.

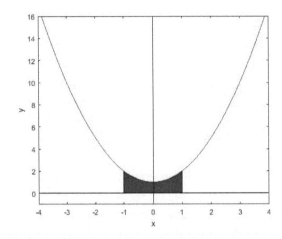

It is pretty obvious that there is no way one can calculate the area shown in the figure easily. The code below demonstrates how MATLAB will solve this for us:

```
fun   = @( x ) x .^2  + 1

q  =   integral (fun,–1, 1)
```

This is very similar to the previous piece of code we examined, so no explanation is going to be given. The only things that changed are the function definition and the interval over which we are computing the integral.

CHAPTER 7. *DIFFERENTIAL EQUATIONS*

Numerical analysis is also concerned with computing (in an approximate way) the solution of differential equations, both ordinary differential equations and partial differential equations. Partial differential equations are solved by first discretizing the equation, bringing it into a finite-dimensional subspace. This can be done by a finite element method, a finite difference method, or (particularly in engineering) a finite volume method. The theoretical justification of these methods often involves theorems from functional analysis. This reduces the problem to the solution of an algebraic equation.

Many readers may be disturbed by differential equations,and they might have to out-step their comfort zone regarding numerical analysis. Given that, and the fact that this book addresses to beginners, we will just look at 2 trivial examples on how to solve differential equations using MATLAB.

The first differential equation, we are going to handle with MATLAB, is described below:

$$\frac{dy}{dt} = ty \tag{7.1}$$

For those who have a basic knowledge of numerical analysis will already be familiar with this equation. What we see here is a first order linear ordinary differential equation. Below, we demonstrate the MATLAB code that will solve this equation:

```
syms y ( t )
ode = d i ff ( y , t ) == t * y ;
ySol = dsolve ( ode ) ;
```

Let's start analyzing this code. The first line creates a new symbolic function. This is different from what we saw before, regarding symbolic variables.

The (t) denotes that this symbolic variable is going to be used for a differential equation. Next, we define the equation using == and represent differentiation using the $diff$ function. This is similar to how we defined the equations in chapter 3. The last step is to use $dsolve$ to solve this differential equation. The result we are going to get is:

$$y = ce^{\frac{t^2}{2}} \tag{7.2}$$

The constant c appears because we have no initial conditions specified.

The next differential equation we are going to tackle using MATLAB is the one described below:

$$\frac{d^2y}{dx^2} = \cos(2x) - y$$

(7.3)   This equation is a second order ordinary differential equation. In order not to have a constant c like before and for demonstrating purposes, we will set the following initial conditions:

$$y(0) = 1$$
$$y'(0) = 0$$

(7.4)

MATLAB will handle this differential equation similarly to the previous one:

```
syms y ( x )
Dy = d i f f( y );
```

```
ode = d i ff ( y , x , 2 ) == cos ( 2 * x ) – y ;

cond1 = y ( 0 ) == 1 ;

cond2 = Dy( 0 ) == 0 ;

conds = [ cond1 cond2 ] ;

ySol ( x ) = dsolve ( ode , conds )
```

Again, we create the symbolic variable $y(x)$. Due to the fact that we have initial conditions, we differentiate once the symbolic variable, thus creating Dy. Next, we create the ordinary differential equation the same way we did in the previous example. Please, take note of the third parameter of the function *diff*. This means that we have a second order equation. After doing that we set the initial conditions that were given to us and we put them in a vector. Finally, we use the function *dsolve* to solve this differential equation.

One extra parameter we use is the one describing the initial conditions. There is not much point in showing the final result since it is a long and trivial solution.

This is all we are going to talk about when it comes to differential equations. Of course, this is a vast area that takes lots of practicing before feeling comfortable in it.

CONCLUSION.

Here, we reached the end of this e-book. I hope that all readers feel a little bit more confident using MATLAB to tackle numerical analysis problems.

I think that it is pretty clear now how helpful MATLAB can be to give fast and easy solutions to severe problems. Of course, this e-book only covered the basics of numerical analysis and MATLAB. There are many more interesting subjects of numerical analysis that can be studied. Even that this area is vast, MATLAB will always be here, helping us.

THANK YOU BUT CAN I ASK YOU FOR A FAVOR?

Let me say thank you for downloading and reading my book. This would be all about. Hope you enjoyed it but you need to keep on learning to be perfect! If you enjoyed this book, found it useful or otherwise then I'd really grateful it if you would post a short review on Amazon. I read all the reviews personally so I can get your feedback and make this book even better.

Thanks for your support!